How to Start Forex Trading Online

The Complete Guide to Becoming a Trader Starting Completely from Zero. Included Approved and Easily Replicable Strategies

John Fazio

Copyright

© Copyright 2024 – John Fazio

original author of this work can in any way be held responsible for any difficulty or damage that may happen to them after undertaking the information described here.

In addition, the information on the following pages is intended for informational purposes only and should therefore be regarded as universal. As befits its nature, they are presented without assurance regarding their prolonged validity or provisional quality. Trademarks that are mentioned are made without written consent and can in no way be considered an endorsement by the trademark owner.

§§§

Printing and distribution: tredition GmbH, An der Strusbek 10, 22926 Ahrensburg - Germany

INDEX

TRADING ONLINE: FROM 0 TO TRADER

CHAPTER 1: WHAT IS THE STOCK MARKET

In any business deal or commercial venture, preparation and knowledge are the keys to success. Without this kind of insight, attempting to make a profitable financial decision can only end in disaster and failure, regardless of your level of motivation and determination or the amount of money you plan to invest.

In the stock market, this rule applies to the nth degree, since you are investing your money in what could be considered a high-risk bet, and you are playing with fire if you do not have at least a general basic understanding of how it works. Since having a background in any area is useful in guiding you along a path in that particular region, the more solid your investment knowledge base, the more likely you are to profit from any attempt to trade on the open market.

In many ways, stock market trading can be compared to driving-you do not need to be an expert to get behind the wheel of a car, although you are expected to have some prior knowledge of basic traffic laws, including moving violations, safety rules, and other legal vehicle infractions, which are learned either through specific study and courses or even through some form of simple exposure (such as the years you spent riding horses with your parents and others who have been driving for years). You should be able to understand the basic tools used to navigate a car (where the brake pedal is in relation to the gas, and how to use the rearview mirror, for example), even if you have never touched a steering wheel.

The same applies to entering the world of the stock market. While it is not necessary to know all the terminology (you will not be selling short or determining your long and short positions at first, so it is not necessary to completely understand these references, although you should be aware of them), you should certainly be familiar with the basic functionality of trading stocks, bonds, bonds and other commodities. And just like someone who is behind the wheel of a car and getting ready to touch the gas pedal for the first time, you should start carefully and work your way up slowly. First-time drivers will first set the mirrors to their liking, then put the car in gear, look for any interference with traffic, and mellow out on the accelerator pedal, never putting it down and test the engine coming out of the gate on the first try. Similarly, when selecting your first investment, you should choose something stable with few fluctuations and not invest a large sum of money in this first venture.

When a person is learning to drive, they will be accompanied by another individual who has more experience and can assist them in making better driving decisions and offering corrections that will help them learn to handle the car more efficiently. In the stock market, there are stockbrokers and other experts who can give you input and advice to help you build your knowledge of the commodities in which you are interested, essentially "guiding" you toward better buying and selling decisions in the stock market.

You could spend hours researching the stock market and its functionality, learning how to get involved in the trade and who to contact to get in the game, especially if your interest is the foreign exchange market, which goes far beyond the level of complication of the domestic stock market. However, in this book, you will find all the basic information you need to get started on the road to trading success. All the legwork and research has been done for you, gathering the data and knowledge into a single source from which you can get enough information to make you a successful trader in the open market. All you have to do is read to gain knowledge and wisdom, step by step, that will take you to a heady level of success. In this book, you will find all this useful information, all brought together in one source for ease of reference.

How the investment works

Whenever you put your money into a fund, it is a good idea to start by understanding what you are buying into. The stock market is a complicated entity, and doing minimal business in trading requires a fair amount of basic knowledge, as well as understanding and accepting the high risk factor. The more you know in advance about the functionality of the system, the less likely you are to take a heavy hit, ending in a devastating loss.

First of all, and probably most important in the business of trading, you should understand what stocks actually are. When you buy or sell a stock on the open market, you should keep in mind that you are dealing with real objects, not pieces of paper; you are buying and selling real parts of a particular company, its product, or some other miscellaneous commodity.

Owning a "share" means that you have actually bought the company or product in question and have become a partial owner of that asset. Of course, you might be one of millions of shareholders, since most companies and products are broken down into tiny pieces of the whole, but you are still considered an investor in that company or product until you sell your shares.

Think of it as paying for a tank of gas in the car your parents bought for you to drive. You may also have bought the oil filter that was put on the car, and you may think that this investment makes you part owner. However, when you look at the total cost of the car, you have really contributed very little to this amount. However, as long as you continue to invest in gas for the car and take care of maintenance needs, you can claim partial ownership of the car.

Because the value of a company and its products or services can fluctuate continuously, the value of the shares you own will not be the same from one day to the next and sometimes can even change hourly. When the price per share falls and is considered low, it is an ideal time to buy. This is the least expensive way to begin your trading adventure, and working with a stock broker will allow you to get more information about which stocks are ripe for purchase at any given time.

By doing so, you become a shareholder, and the value of your holdings will fluctuate from day to day. Your bet (and hope!) is that the value of the company or product you have invested in will increase or rebound from the low price at which you made your purchase. This is the goal of all traders and means that your stock will be more valuable.

As the value of your securities increases, so does your net worth. When the price of the shares you own reaches a high point, it is time to sell, making a profit on your original investment. Ideally, you will always sell your holdings at a price reasonably higher than your purchase amount, and you should never sell when the current value of the shares is less than your initial purchase price. It is important to make sure that you do not intentionally take a net loss because there are many occasions when you might be forced to take a loss.

For example, if you buy shares in a company at twenty dollars each, you should never sell them at eighteen dollars each. If possible, you want to wait until they are worth perhaps forty dollars each, essentially doubling your money. Of course, this is just one example, and not every stock will ever double in value, but the illustration is significant.

There are other more complex ways to invest in the stock market. However, just like learning to ride a bicycle, it is best not to make the first attempt without training wheels.

How to Make Decisions at the Beginning

We return to the guide as a reference. When you start driving, you do not enter the highway and drive your car at speeds of sixty and seventy kilometers per hour. Instead, you will stay in residential areas or at least on the access road, where there is less pressure to maintain such a high speed. In the stock market, you will also want to stay away from any expensive stocks or extremely volatile investments until you have become extremely comfortable with the trading process.

There are small investment opportunities called "penny stocks" that will help you try your sea legs and get a feel for how the stock market works before you invest large sums of money and risk a big financial loss. These particular stocks literally cost pennies or small dollar amounts and typically fluctuate only fractions of a cent on any given day, making them extremely safe for those just getting started.

Once you get the hang of it and can better judge market trends, you can comfortably move on to more complicated and adventurous areas of the market. It is like taking the training wheels off your bicycle or entering the highway for the first time at a time of day when there is no traffic to contend with.

Be aware that just as you can fall off your bicycle once or twice and end up with a few scrapes and bruises, you can lose money in an investment here and there. This is very typical, and investing in the stock market is very similar to gambling. In poker, you cannot expect to win every hand, and the same is true in the investment world. Learning to watch market trends, however, is similar to watching other cars as you join traffic and determine the correct speed and proximity to other cars for optimal safety. Such diligent study can help you drastically improve your statistics in a short time.

CHAPTER 2: STOCK MARKET TRENDS

Understanding stock market trends can make your job of making money in the market much easier. Conversely, if you know little or nothing about these trends it can cause serious losses.

Bulls and bears

As we dig deeper into the market and learn more about how it works, we begin to hear certain terms about marketing trends that seem to be repeated over and over again. Market trends are variable and volatile, both on a daily basis and over extended periods of time. In the past, for example, the United States has had devastating stock market crashes, but because of the freedom of a capitalist society, the U.S. economy has always rebounded in the end.

What does the rebound in the market or a particular stock mean? Assuming that the value of a company or its stock has plummeted to a level that seems irretrievable, leaving it virtually worthless, one may get the impression that that company is in danger of bankruptcy and of leaving the reach of free trade markets altogether. Suddenly, however, the founder of that company can introduce a new product for which consumers go crazy. Everyone wants one, and this product can become scarce at the time of its introduction, causing a rush to department store shelves.

When such a move occurs, the law of supply and demand will take over, making the company valuable again. The stock price of that company will recover, and the resulting gain in value will be considered a rebound-a return to the original (or better) state before the devastating loss.

The market tends upward or downward, and there are specific references to strong changes in market values that are often heard. If several areas of the market are in a steep decline, with values falling rapidly (perhaps as much as ten or twenty percent in a few days), this is called a bear market. You may recall this reference as being in the extremely dangerous position of being chased by a bear-if you are in possession of several stocks or other assets that are worth a good amount, you have a serious chance of losing a large amount of value that could translate into a net loss of value if you choose to sell, and it can be a similar, very dangerous situation.

The best thing in such cases is to sell before prices fall below the original purchase price or hold the stock until the market recovers. However, when the bear market reaches a low point, it may be an ideal time to enter the game, as it is rare for prices to fall below this point. Then, if you wait patiently for the market to recover or rebound, you can make a great deal of money from a bear market. These options will be discussed in more detail in later chapters.

At the same time, a bull market is a strong general upward trend for many stocks. One could compare this to the running of the bulls in Pamplona, Spain, every year. You are safer if you are covered when the run occurs, and by the same token, if you own stocks during a bull market, you are in a prime position to increase your net worth and sell your stocks, making a large amount of money. This is another idea that will be further explored in detail later in this book.

The market outlook

By taking note of the various changes in the status of the different stock options available, you will learn how to spot early market trends, giving you a clue as to the future of a particular commodity, and this can only add to your chances of profitability. Forecasting is a big part of the game when working in the stock market, since you can never be completely certain in which direction the market will swing at any given time.

However, an educated guess can be made, just like a weatherman making weather forecasts. Even if he or she is not right 100 percent of the time, the forecast is usually pretty close to the actual weather outcome because the forecaster is a scientist who has studied weather trends and can pick up on the details that help make that educated guess. With some time and seasoning, you can achieve the same level of experience and insight in the stock market.

Once you have become more comfortable operating in the same world as stockbrokers and day traders, and feel confident (or at least less nervous or self-conscious) about making such important financial decisions, you may decide to make your move into the Foreign Exchange Market (more commonly known as Forex), and the goal of this book is to prepare you to operate within the confines of this more complex entity. Next, we will discuss some of the properties of Forex and how much more complex this stock market entity can be than a standard domestic market.

The Foreign Exchange Market is incredibly volatile, and there are many more factors to consider when placing an order on this market than on a domestic market. The following chapter is an introduction to the exciting and somewhat scary world of the Foreign Exchange Market, or Forex.

CHAPTER 3: INTRODUCTION TO FOREX

Forex is the nickname for the foreign exchange market. In the United States, there are several branches of the stock market, each with its own name. For example, some stocks trade on the Dow Jones, others on the Nasdaq. Of course, all stock market transactions in the United States take place on the New York Stock Exchange (NYSE). In other countries it is the same. There may be one or more distinct markets.

However, international trade takes place in the market called the Foreign Exchange Market, or Forex. Several countries around the world, in almost all time zones, participate in Forex trading, using multiple currencies and offering stocks and commodities from all participating countries. Because there are so many nations and time zones involved, Forex does not function as a "business day" entity like most domestic stock markets. It remains open for business 24 hours a day, 5 days a week.

Of course, these additional hours intensely increase the risk factor for those of us who are human and obviously cannot monitor our investments 24 hours a day. This means that the value of your holdings could potentially plummet overnight while you sleep because other countries are still trading while you are in dreamland. Again, it's like a car-there are many moving parts under the hood, and just because you can't see them doesn't mean they're not working.

This is one reason for several security options, such as limit orders, which we will discuss later. This is also why it is strongly recommended that your first attempts to make money in the stock market should not be transactions that take place within the

Foreign Exchange Market but on a standard nine-to-five domestic trading market. In our automotive analogy, this would be comparable to asking someone who has never driven or even changed the oil in a car to rebuild the engine.

Forex functionality

While the functionality of Forex is the same as a domestic exchange, commodities and prices are more volatile, and there are additional factors to consider in addition to the typical risks associated with a domestic market. You will have to contend not only with the value of your stocks and currency, but also with the foreign currencies involved in any Forex trade or exchange, as well as inconsistencies in the values of particular goods and services across international borders. It is like driving a car with a standard transmission instead of an automatic. On the inside front, the work is largely done for you, and all you have to do is navigate, just like an automatic transmission. However, changing gears is quite similar to having to constantly participate in currency conversion. It can be distracting, and it certainly complicates the act of driving.

Since the financial situation of many countries is not as secure as that of the United States, this can be a formidable problem in determining where to invest one's money and what to expect next in the international market. Knowing which countries and currencies are involved in Forex can help you by allowing you to monitor more closely the financial situation in the nations with which you will interact.

The history of Forex

When foreign trade began, it was not an international trade market. It was born out of the Bretton Woods Agreement of 1944, which stipulated that foreign currencies would be fixed against the dollar, which was valued at $35 per ounce of gold. This precedent was first put into practice in 1967, when a Chicago bank refused to finance a loan to a professor in sterling. Of course, his intention was to sell the currency, which he believed was priced too high against the dollar, and then buy it back later when the value dropped, making a quick profit.

After 1971, when the dollar was no longer convertible to gold and the domestic market was stronger, the Bretton Woods agreement was abandoned and the currency conversion process became more variable. This allowed stronger support in foreign markets, and the United States and Europe began a strong trade relationship. In the 1980s, market time and use was expanded through the use of computers and technology to include Asian time zones. At that time, foreign exchange was about $70 billion a day. Today, some two decades later, the level of trading has skyrocketed, with trading at about $1.5 trillion a day.

Originally, trading across international lines was more difficult, with several different currencies involved throughout Europe. Although the major players in the European market were deeply involved and veterans of international trade when other markets joined, there were more currencies to keep track of-the franc, the pound, the lira and many others-than was reasonable. With the birth of the European Union in 1992, the wheels were set in motion to create a single currency that would be used in most of Europe, and the euro was finally established and put into circulation in 1999.

Forex Today

While some countries have not yet accepted the currency as their own (such as Great Britain, which still uses the pound sterling), the currency conversion process has been simplified without the large number of various currencies that people had to deal with before. Instead of dozens of currencies, major countries trade in five: U.S. dollars, Australian dollars, British pounds, euros and Japanese yen.

Today, the foreign exchange market is international and global. The market is open 24 hours a day, 5 days a week, to accommodate all time zones of all major players. These now include most of Europe, the United States, and Asian markets, especially Japan. Australia has also joined international trade markets, and since these nations are halfway around the world from some of the other top players, time zones must obviously be taken into account.

Another completely separate but perhaps more important concern for Forex trading is understanding how trading in multiple currencies works. How can you compare the value of a stock across international lines if the values are expressed in two separate, non-equivalent currencies? And how do you measure gains and losses when the conversion rate is constantly changing?

CHAPTER 4: UNDERSTAND CURRENCY CONVERSION

When you start trading Forex, you have to learn how to convert currencies and notice the difference in values, as well as how currencies are traded across international lines. This means studying not only domestic market trends and currency values, but also those of foreign markets.

Operating with multiple currencies

Since Forex is the foreign exchange market, obviously you cannot expect everyone within the market to trade in U.S. dollars (and why not, you might ask? - but remember that not everyone wants the U.S. dollar). With so many variables and volatile currencies being traded, how can you recognize a good buy or sell when you see one without complete awareness of the value of the foreign currency?

The first step is to find a source that gives you a basic idea of the current exchange rate between your domestic currency and the foreign currency in question. You should do this as a basic list for any currency you might be involved with. Of course, this will not be consistent down to the penny or fraction of a particular currency during an entire business day, but at least you will have your starting point to begin with, almost like North on a compass. Such sources can be found on the Internet, as well as through many brokers, both online and in person.

Currency conversion

It is also good to understand the medium by which currency conversion is expressed. The comparison is usually made in a report known as a cross rate. In this configuration, the two currencies are listed in a XXX/YYYY ratio, with position XXX listed as the base currency. The base currency is usually expressed as a whole number, while the YYYY position is expressed as the decimal that is closest to the base currency rate. It is a bit like referring to miles per gallon or rpm on a car-a direct comparison of one to the other in the form of a ratio.

The smallest fraction, or decimal, in which a currency can be traded is called a pip, and this is usually the degree to which a cross rate is expressed. For example, if the British pound can be traded in thousandths, the currency will be expressed to the third decimal place. The U.S. dollar is often expressed to the hundredth of a cent (the fourth decimal place).

In an example of a cross-rate expression, one U.S. dollar may be equivalent to 117.456 Japanese yen. This ratio would be expressed as 1,000/117,456. The base currency is almost always expressed as a single unit (such as one dollar versus ten dollars), and often that unit is the U.S. dollar. Because the value of the whole number (or large digit, as it is called) of the secondary currency, or the currency in the YYYY position in terms of conversion changes so infrequently, often only the decimal part of the number is mentioned in the Foreign Exchange Market.

Therefore, in the above report, it can be heard that the yen is trading at .456, with no mention of the full 117 yen that is shown in the report. This is because the exchange rate can vary from 117.456 to 117.423, but not to 119.024. Experiencing a change in the large digit-the whole number in front of the decimal-unless it was only because the number was already within a few thousandths, would represent too large a shift in value for a single trading period and would be a rare event that could cause the entire market to swing dramatically in one direction or the other.

The most common currencies found in Forex are the U.S. dollar, British pound sterling, euro, Japanese yen, and Australian dollar. In the past, there would have been many other currencies to keep track of (such as the franc, lira or German mark). However, with the consolidation of most of the European Forex trading market to the Euro, many currencies have been eliminated, making Forex trading for other lands less complicated.

If you buy a commodity in a particular currency, and the value of that currency falls against the U.S. dollar, you can actually make money by selling that same commodity in dollars. The same is true in reverse if the value of a foreign currency increases against the U.S. dollar. Of course, it is only possible to take advantage of such a situation if the goods are traded in both currencies and in both markets in question. We will discuss this process, as well as other ways to take advantage of the Foreign Exchange Market (such as arbitrage) in more detail in future chapters.

Once you are able to discern a base value of any particular currency and its conversion rate relative to others traded on Forex, you will be able to more closely monitor the change in currency conversion, including its inconsistency and volatility. These ideas will not seem so "foreign" to you, and you will be involved and aware right along with the professionals. Then, you will have to learn how to read, understand and eventually interpret further market trends.

Forex Trend

Following charts, listening to advice from market analysts and chartists, and learning to make educated forecasts yourself will help you keep track of various market trends. The next chapter will explain more about using published statistics to predict the next move in the stock market. Will it be a clear and calm day with little activity, or is there a storm coming with winds of change and uncertainty? How can you tell what will happen with your participations the next day or even further into the future?

Simply learning to read market trends can eliminate a lot of apprehension and uncertainty natural to beginning traders. In fact, sometimes the best first step to enter the market is to watch programs about it or read the financial sections of newspapers that detail trends and expected outcomes. The following chapter will better explain how to interpret basic statistics and trends.

CHAPTER 5: UNDERSTAND STATISTICS

You are now familiar with how the stock market works, and you understand to a certain extent what trading in the foreign exchange market entails. Now, you would like to know how to assess market trends to profit from your business ventures in the open market. We are no longer talking about penny stocks and playground games. You want the real thing.

The name of the game is statistics, and the first rule is that you should be aware that there is no such thing as a sure thing in the stock market. While you can never be 100 percent sure at any time of the next move that will be made in the market as a whole, being able to read statistics and interpret them will put you ahead of the pack as far as "guessing" what will happen next.

Investing is very similar to gambling. If you can keep track of the cards that have already been played, you are more informed, statistically, about what is likely to be dealt later, which means you can bet with greater insight than someone who has no idea what has already been played. With the market open, if you have information about what has already occurred in the last few days, months or even years, you are again in a better position to more logically conclude what will happen next. You simply learn the pattern and follow it to the end, reaping the financial rewards.

Charts

Wait, you thought you had to research and track the market's past all by yourself? Of course not! There are people who are paid to do this kind of work. They monitor the market every hour, every day, every week, every month, and every year so that they can provide high-level traders with the same knowledge mentioned earlier. The more an investment company knows about the market, the more money it can make. The same applies to stockbrokers. They make money when you make money, and they want to do the best they can to make sure you make smart decisions.

The best part of this is that you have access to the same information as these VIP clients. Chartists, who are essentially market analysts publishing their results in easy-to-read charts, produce what is called a candlestick chart. These charts are basically a combination of a line graph and a bar graph that show the trend of various stocks, indexes, or other interests over a given period of time. Therefore, it is easy to determine whether the commodity is in an upward trend or taking a downturn, when the last major change occurred, and how long the stock or bond is expected to continue on the current path.

One can actually find information on most commodities and their market trends for years in the past, and some even up to their introduction to the open market. Using this information can help you decide whether it is a good idea to buy or sell the stocks or securities in which you have an interest, or whether it is better to wait for a spike in the market trend.

Understanding market trends

Understandably, as economies change, the value of various commodities may change. This is because when an economy is strong and thriving, a nation is wealthier and has more purchasing power. Along with this power comes a higher value for purchased items. In other words, if people have more money to spend and spend more in Walmart stores, the value of Walmart's stock will multiply at a considerable rate. Therefore, shareholders become wealthier in terms of assets, simply because buyers are driving the market with their purchasing power. When shareholders are rich, and the value of their holdings is rising, they continue to buy stocks, which again, pump up the economy. A strong upward trend in the stock market is a very good sign for any economy.

However, there are also things that affect the market in a negative way, causing the value of stocks to fall. For example, war rarely has a positive effect on the stock market. On September 11, 2001, when terrorists attacked the World Trade Center in New York, the U.S. economy suffered a huge collapse and the nation was threatened with a depression. Some analysts were sure that it would never recover properly. The same thing typically happens whenever there is an attack or act of war within a nation. However, the critics proved them wrong, and the United States proceeded to rebound, or recover from a bad downward trend, in a strong way. This rapid recovery occurred mainly because the people of the United States continued to push and spend, forcing money and wealth back into the economy. By watching the reaction of the stock market, one can learn to read trends based on world events.

Oil prices also commonly influence the stock market. Especially in the foreign exchange market, you will find that trends vary depending on many current events. You will also note that, over time, the principal value (or face value) of a currency may be deliberately revised by a nation in terms of currency conversion. This is called devaluation, which will be discussed in more detail in the following chapter.

CHAPTER 6: FOREX VOLATILITY AND MARKET EXPECTATIONS

Volatility, or the tendency for fluctuation that can affect your gains within the stock market, is typical within a domestic market but even more evident and much stronger on the Foreign Exchange Market. What factors affect the value of currency on Forex, and is there any way to control it?

Depreciation and revaluation

As mentioned in the previous chapter, devaluation refers to the intentional decline in the value of a currency in relation to other currencies as required by a government agency. For example, if the U.S. dollar is worth ten units of a foreign currency that is then devalued by ten percent, the U.S. dollar is now equivalent to only nine units of the foreign currency. This makes any item purchased in the foreign currency more expensive for those trading in U.S. dollars as the exchange rate falls. It also makes items in the foreign country less expensive to exchange into U.S. dollars.

An opposite change in value may also occur, increasing the value of the foreign currency. This is called revaluation. Although it may seem that purposely adjusting the value of a nation's currency is "cheating," or taking an unfair advantage by making foreign products cheaper to buy and increasing the value of exports, there are regulations in place to prevent the manipulation of exchange rates for such purposes. IMF (International Monetary Fund) bylaws help prohibit such events and enforce the policy.

There are ways in which one can benefit from devaluation and revaluation, which will be discussed later. However, what happens when the value of a foreign currency changes due to market fluctuation rather than intentional reductions or increases by a federal government or federal bank? How do appreciation and depreciation affect the stock market?

Appreciation and depreciation

Depreciation can easily be related to the life of a car. As soon as you drive a new car off the lot, the value is almost halved. This is extreme depreciation. However, in the coming years, the car continues to lose value at a more gradual pace. This is also considered depreciation.

Currency appreciation and depreciation are changes in the value of the currency that are driven by market forces rather than government mandate. For example, in an effort to repay some loans, in 1998 the Central Bank of Russia announced the upcoming devaluation of the ruble. The exchange rate, which was currently six rubles per U.S. dollar, would rise in a period of time to 9.5 rubles per dollar, effectively a depreciation of 34 percent.

However, before the change, there was widespread panic in the former communist nation, and the value of the ruble fell due to many people in Russia choosing to trade their bonds before the deadline. In just one day after the announcement, the Russian ruble depreciated by an incredible 25 percent.

The same kind of crisis occurred in the 1920s with the collapse of the U.S. stock market. At that time, panic spread nationwide, and people rushed to banks to withdraw cash that was not available or to exchange securities and stock options that had not matured. By running to the bank, people actually caused the collapse rather than escaping from it.

On the other side of the coin, too rapid an appreciation predisposes a country to inflation, or an increase in the retail value of products sold to the public based on currency valuation. Although inflation is bound to occur, it can be minimally mitigated through the use of currency valuation.

Appreciation can also be tied to a vehicle. Often, men enjoy taking old cars and restoring them to their original beauty. By doing so, they dramatically increase the value of the vehicle or appreciate it.

The ever-changing currency conversion rates and market volatility create inherent market risk, or a day-to-day potential to suffer losses due to fluctuating security prices. There is no way to diversify this type of risk, as it will always affect investments to some extent. However, some risks may be offset by particular types of investments or ways of investing that are safer or protected.

We will take a look at long and short positions, short selling, stop orders and other ways to protect your investments from drastic losses in later chapters. These options include the ability to preset the buy or sell price for a specific commodity, as well as the use of various predetermined order levels to place orders and complete transactions.

Of course, do not delude yourself that you can get rid of all possible risk factors in the market. There is always a cloud hanging over your head waiting to burst, and all it takes is a little pinprick. You must always exercise caution, even though the idea of playing in the stock market inherently involves danger and excitement. The next chapter will help you understand reality and what is involved in balancing your risk factor with a grounding in reality; your ego with your id.

CHAPTER 7: ASPECTS OF TRADE

You now know the functionality of the stock market and have decided that you are willing to accept the risk factors involved. However, you want to know all you can about how to balance that risk with smart investment options. How can you be sure that the risks you take are more likely to be rewarding in the long run than destructive?

Long and short

One of the most important parts of making money in the stock market is determining your position. The long position is basically the buy position-you are about to make a long-term commitment to ownership of some stock, security, or other traded commodity. The short position, on the contrary, is the selling position-you are about to dispose of the same kind of property and any liability to it.

The best time to take a long position is when stock prices are low. This will get you into the market at a reasonable price and increase your chances of profit when new bids go up in price and old investment options recover or rebound. In fact, when others take the long position and buy at the same time you do, this will cause the value of stocks to rise through the standard rule of supply and demand, causing the beginning of what could be a bull market.

One can equate this situation to the end of the month at a car dealership. Prices tend to fall on all cars left for sale, and the dealer is more often willing to haggle because he wants less inventory on the lot. Similarly, when stock prices are low, some people panic and dump all their holdings at these low prices, thinking that their shares will never recover value. This can only help you.

When prices are high, it is likely to be time to turn around and sell one's shares to make a profit, without losing anything on the unrealized gain (profit that cannot be counted in liquid assets or cash because it is still invested in a volatile stock option). You should never sell for less than your cost, because this brings negative equity and a loss of funds. One should always sell for the maximum profit that is deemed safe.

In other words, if you buy a stock at fifteen dollars per share, and it quickly rises to twenty-five dollars per share, you may well think it could reach thirty dollars per share within a week. However, you need to determine whether you are willing to risk losing your already-insured earnings of ten dollars per share to wait that long, should the price actually fall; then, you might decide to sell at the current high price.

Market-Maker and short selling

What happens if stock values are incredibly high, but you haven't entered that particular commodity and you don't own stocks? Your first step should be to visit a market-maker or make an agreement with a broker for a short sale. A market-maker is literally a stockbroker who buys keeps on hand a certain amount of shares of different securities or stocks, which are purchased during a period when market rates are low.

The company will then turn around and sell those shares to an individual at that low price, regardless of the market rate, in effect making its own market (hence the name). The individual who buys from the company can immediately sell the commodities on the open market at the market rate (which is higher), making an incredible amount of profit in a short period of time.

A short sale is another option for a quick profit. In this scenario, you will borrow a particular number of shares from a broker to sell when the market value is high. Your job is to wait for the stock price to fall, buy the same amount of stock, and return the holdings to the broker, keeping the profit from the sale, minus the broker's commission.

The way a car dealer works with trade-ins is very similar. They will buy the car from you at a very low price, then turn around and sell it on the lot for a high profit margin.

One of the most positive aspects of a short sale is that you never actually take possession of the stock, which means you are never likely to lose money. Because you sold the stock at a high price, you have already made a profit, and in the worst case scenario, the stock in question will not drop in price. Rather than returning the shares to the broker from whom they were borrowed, one can simply repay the amount for which they were originally purchased, along with the premium.

How can you be sure that you will not outperform the best price options or lose a good rate because you are not available to place a buy or sell order with your broker? Is there any way to set limits on your exchanges? Next, we will discuss ways to protect your investments and limit your risk factors.

CHAPTER 8: RISK MANAGEMENT

One of the most important aspects of protecting your investments is balancing risk with reassurance. There are several ways to do this, and we will discuss them in this chapter.

Limit orders and balancing risks

A limit order is a fixed amount at which you have agreed to buy or sell a particular security or other commodity. For example, you have indicated to your stockbroker that you will not sell security X until its value reaches a minimum value of Y dollars. At the same time, you will not buy the same security X if it exceeds a value of Z. Setting limits on the price you pay for a particular security, as well as the price you will accept to sell it, protects you and your investment in several ways.

First of all, you are maximizing your gains, but more importantly, you are avoiding losses. Any loss that occurs with limit orders will always be an unrealized loss, or a loss that is not measurable in liquid assets or cash. In other words, as long as you do not sell the stock and collect the net loss, it will not affect your net worth. Because you have set a limit that does not allow you to sell your raw materials for less than original cost, you may not have a loss in your net worth. At the same time, you are also securing at least a certain amount of profit by setting your selling point high enough to reap that particular profit.

Another way to protect your assets is through hedging. This means that you create and sell a futures contract in which you state that when the stock reaches a certain value in the future, you will sell your holdings at this predetermined price. When that price is reached, the order will be processed and the transaction completed. Of course, if you ever change your mind about a limit you set, you can place a stop order with your broker, which designates that you no longer wish to trade at the specified dollar amount.

It can also be bought on the margin. This is very similar to short selling, but instead of borrowing shares to sell them, you are essentially borrowing money to buy shares on your own when the market value is falling. Then, when the value of the securities you bought goes up and you are able to sell at a profit, you repay the loan and keep the excess from the sale, minus the broker's commissions. Of course, all dealings with a stockbroker involve a premium, or a fee for services rendered, and it is almost impossible to trade without a broker or broker service. However, online services are often less expensive than in-person agents, but you can do some research to determine which is your best option.

How can I handle a whip?

No, we are not referring to something in the garage, bedroom, or country band. A whipsaw is a market trend that defies the odds. It can be thought of as the "fender." Despite how carefully you learn to drive a car and become coordinated, sometimes there is nothing you can do to avoid being rear-ended.

Whipsaw is a term for what happens when everything points toward a specific direction in the market trend, causing you to buy (if it looks like prices are about to go up) or sell (if it looks like they are about to go down), then the opposite effect occurs.

For example, if you buy a stock at five dollars per share because the stock seems to have fallen to the top and seems to start an upward trend, then unexpectedly the stock collapses to one dollar per share, this is considered a whiplash effect. If this happens to you, as it surely will if you play the market long enough, the best thing to do is to wait. The stock will do one of two things--either it will dissolve completely, and the company will go bankrupt (this is what you don't want to happen), or it will rebound, and you can choose to wait for a chance to make a profit or you can get out as soon as the buy rate is reached.

Lashings are not the end of the world, and no one can expect to make money with every purchase on the stock market. However, if you find that you are involved in several of these cases, you should seriously reconsider your investment options. It is possible that you are reading the signals incorrectly, or that you are choosing bad actions. You should seek advice for any future investments you plan to make before buying more stocks or securities.

Another way to reverse a bad investment like this is to proceed with an offsetting transaction-a purchase or sale that offsets the loss of a previous transaction. You could buy more shares of the same company at the lower price if you expect it to recover, or you could opt for another hot commodity that is about to explode in price, both of which will help offset your loss. You might also sell shares of a security in which you have a large amount of unrealized gain-gain that cannot be measured in liquid assets or cash because of the increase in value of the shares and securities held-in order to replace the lost cash value.

All of these are good options for recovering a loss, but waiting for the stock value to rebound is always the first choice. It avoids the loss of already invested funds, maintains the possibility of pursuing profit, and reduces the risk of further investment in the market.

CHAPTER 9: KEY WORDS TO KNOW

Now that you know a little more about the stock market, and have decided to try your hand at investing, you should be more concerned about understanding the jargon you will hear on the trading floor. While you probably won't be among a bunch of screaming stockbrokers on Wall Street (and these days, most trading is done on a computer anyway), know that learning to talk is part of walking.

Margin, spread and other terms

Okay, it's about margins, not margarine, but it sounds very similar. To understand the stock market, especially on Forex, it is necessary to speak not a language intended for common communication, but the language of trade. For example, when we think of a margin, for many this means a variable-such as the "margin of error" in a statistic.

However, in trading, it refers to the amount of money borrowed from a broker in order to buy stocks when the market is down. Then, when the value starts its next rise, you sell the stock at the higher price, pay back the margin (along with the accrued premium), and keep the profit.

When buying on margin, the money lent by the stockbroker is called a margin account. The margin account is provisional, based on share value. Occasionally, if the value of the shares purchased falls too low for the margin of safety established by the broker, the agent will require more money to be deposited into the margin account to offset the loss. This is called a margin call.

In some exchanges, market value does not come into play. For example, a forward exchange is set up between two individuals or two companies outside the open market. It involves a negotiation process and possible compromise on price. Usually there is an offer made-the offer to buy a commodity at a certain price-and an asking price or bid-the price at which the other business entity is willing to sell the securities or other holdings. The difference between these two purchase numbers is called the spread.

If the spread cannot be narrowed and eventually closed, no deal can be made. This agreed upon price is called the forward price, and all the details involved in the trading process when this type of transaction takes place are detailed in a contract and called forward points. Usually, the forward price is outlined as available for a particular date, and if the transaction is not completed on that date (referred to as the transaction date), then the exchange must be renegotiated.

Jobbers, Yards, and other "British" terms.

One of the main foreign markets that Americans trading Forex will encounter is the British market. While many other terms related to the stock market will be similar because of common language, there are some specific terms that are very different in British trading vocabulary.

For example, in the United States, stockbrokers who hold securities purchased at low prices for the purpose of selling them to customers in a market with higher prices (so that the customer can turn around and sell them back for profit in the open market) are called market-makers. However, in Britain, this type of investor is simply called a "jobber."

Another term you will want to be familiar with is "yard." This does not refer to a piece of green land, a measurement in inches, or even 36 of something. The term is used in reference to quantity of currency rather than value and is equivalent to one million units of the currency in question. In other words, you can have a meter of dollars or a meter of yen, and even though it is the same amount of bills, coins, or any other physical currency used, it is not necessarily equivalent in value.

In Britain they do not use the euro and they do not use the U.S. dollar. They chose to still use the pound, a currency that has been used in the country for hundreds of years. However, Britain is currently on a path to make the conversion to the euro within the next five years.

Open and closed

In the stock market, there are various types of orders that can be placed to protect you from making a bad investment or to limit the amount you pay for a certain security or other commodity. For example, if you have made a bad investment and do not want to reinvest in a particular stock, you should sell all the shares in that stock, regardless of whether you suffer a small loss. This action is called closing a position. Conversely, if you are doing well with your investment, you could participate in a rollover, simply reinvesting your gains in additional shares of the stock.

An open order is exactly what it sounds like; it means that the order remains pending until it is executed by your change agent or cancelled by you as a customer. A stop order would cancel any outstanding orders you have placed with your stockbroker. You also have options such as One cancels other orders. These allow you to have interest in different commodities, leaving orders for your stockbroker to buy them all if they fall to a certain price. Then, should one of them reach this preset low price, your stockbroker will follow your direction and invest your money in that particular security, followed by a cancellation of all additional orders.

When a broker gives you an estimate of the price of a particular stock or commodity, it is considered a quote. A quote is never completely accurate and is usually called a spot price, since the value of a security can change in a matter of seconds. However, it is as close to accuracy as can be expected. When you place an order, the broker processes the fill, or completion, of that order.

The actual value at which the transaction is completed is called the fill price. The completion of a trade or purchase, called settlement, may also be called execution of a transaction or realization of an order. As you can see, there are many terms to consider, and we have not even begun to look at the terms used in some of the more difficult areas of the market.

Next, we will consider some specialized and more complex trading options that you can use on Forex to take advantage of market volatility and constantly changing exchange rates.

CHAPTER 10: EXPERT TRADING WITH OPTIONS

After spending a lot of time buying and trading in domestic and foreign markets, you will find that the process becomes easier and almost intuitive. No longer will you have to work so hard to determine currency conversion or find the next big explosive raw material. It will be like second nature to you.

What then becomes the next big challenge for open market traders? What keeps things from becoming monotonous and boring? First of all, there is always something new and different happening on the Foreign Exchange Market. Remember, it operates 24 hours a day, and you never know what you will find when you wake up in the morning. However, there are several ways in which you can take advantage of the variance in currency conversion and the time lag between markets that can affect trading values.

Refereeing

There are some commodities that are traded in multiple currencies on multiple markets on Forex. Although computers have made worldwide communication almost lightning fast these days, all these markets can trade together with fairly equivalent values for securities shared between currencies.

However, the system is not perfect, and value can go up or down in one country and currency before the same change in value reaches another border. Experienced traders have learned to take advantage of this lag in market trend by using a process called arbitrage. In this transaction, you buy a particular stock or security in the market with the lowest price and simultaneously sell the same in a market where the value is higher. The process is a bit complex, so we will use an example. Let us say that one U.S. dollar is equivalent to 0.5 British pounds, which means that everything will be twice as expensive in British pounds.

Now, let's take a look at the price of a stock traded on both markets. If they were equivalent, the stock would trade at two dollars in the United States and one pound in Britain. However, if something happens and the value of stocks falls in Britain, Britain is six hours ahead of the United States, and this drop may not hit the U.S. market immediately.

If the share value falls in Britain to 0.8 pounds, the purchase price is now lower than the dollar price because of currency conversion. In this case, arbitrage would take place when shares of the stock are bought in the British market in pounds sterling and sold in the U.S. market in dollars, benefiting from the slow communication of the falling value of the stock. In fact, you will earn $.40 per share.

Currency conversion volatility

Another way to take advantage of the ever-changing value of each individual currency is to trade on the basis of changing rates. What exactly does it involve? You need to look closely at the changing conversion rates. When a currency conversion rate changes dramatically, it is time to make a move. This is very similar to arbitrage, but the area is much riskier because of the high volatility. For example, if you bought a stock in the previous scenario in the U.S. market for two dollars a share, and suddenly the British pound gains value, dropping to a conversion of only half a pound for every two dollars, you would want to sell your stock in the British market because the value of a pound is higher and now has more purchasing power.

One tip to keep in mind, however, is that it is best to dispose of all liquid foreign currency assets immediately, usually on the same day. We talk about next tomorrow because it takes two or three business days for delivery of foreign currency, and by exchanging the currency for value in stocks on the same business day, we avoid having to take delivery of the currency altogether.

CHAPTER 11: OTHER TRADING OPTIONS

In addition to the expert options described above, there are other nontraditional ways to make money in the stock market. In considering these options, however, you should consider making a career of trading stocks and bonds. Some types of trading are simply not for the faint of heart, and that means you must have complete motivation and an adventurous spirit to take part in these areas of the market. The chances of taking a giant hit and experiencing a big loss are multiplied.

Daily trading

Day traders take some of the biggest risks in the market. Because day traders work with investments that change dramatically in a matter of hours, they are by nature in the lion's den. These stocks are extremely volatile, and for the most part, day trading is a quick way to lose a large amount of money. It is difficult to make a large amount of money in this way, and it is even more difficult to predict the outcome of these daytime stock trading options. One cannot be certain of the overnight position (the net value at which a stockbroker or day trader will open the next morning).

And in Forex, there is little room for day trading, since the market never closes during the work week. In such cases, the day trader needs to set a time limit for getting out, selling all the stocks, so that he can sleep soundly while the world turns and start the next day fresh.

Day trading is very dangerous and is not recommended for newcomers. In fact, it is not recommended at all, and most people who participate in this volatile part of the industry are either extremely seasoned in open market trading, do not consider the risk factors carefully enough before entering this branch of the market, or have enough money that they simply want to try this form of investment and do not worry about losing a good amount.

Secondary markets

Secondary markets are interesting in that they are created by the government to help redistribute money that is used for loans. Fannie Mae and Freddie Mac are two of the main companies from which shares are purchased on a secondary market.

Here's how it works. When a person buys a house, he takes a loan from the bank, usually for about eighty percent of the cost of the house. This is granted, and the house is purchased by the bank for the individual or family, which starts paying the loan to the bank.

Meanwhile, to ensure that money is available in that bank for the next person who needs a mortgage loan, Fannie Mae or Freddie Mac, two entities originally established by the U.S. government, will purchase the loan from the bank. Therefore, the money is returned to the bank for future use.

What do these agencies then do with the deficit they have acquired? They sell it. In the secondary market, they break down the loan into shares that are backed by the loan itself and sell these shares, recovering money from investors. Eventually, these securities mature, probably at the same time as the original loan is paid to the bank, and investors reap the benefits of their investment with the interest earned.

Another way to take advantage of a volatile international stock market is to do a swap. This is the trading of stocks or bonds to take advantage of lower interest rates. For example, if a business entity in Britain holds one bond, and another in Japan holds a different bond, the two commodities can be beneficially traded or sold to each other to save on interest rates if the bond or security currently held is held at a lower interest rate in the opposite market.

For example, let's say one company is holding an "A" bond that is paying only two percent interest in its current market, and another is holding "B" bonds in its market at three percent interest. If bond A is actually paying three percent in the foreign market, and bond B can be cashed in for four percent in the first market, both parties can make more money with a bond exchange. They can mutually benefit from one sale of securities to the other because of a gain of more interest.

If this seems confusing, then perhaps a swap is not in your near future. This is more often worked out among companies in the foreign market rather than individual parties, although with the correct broker, it could be accomplished. However, should you work the deal, you need to know little except that you are looking at a higher profit margin than before, and your broker will take care of the rest.

If you decide to have stock options as a business, you will probably decide to hire a full-time advisor for all your financial needs, including the management of your stock holdings. In fact, when companies are large enough and have a strong enough commercial presence within the market, especially on Forex, you will find that there are entire departments dedicated to maintaining stock options.

CHAPTER 12: IN REVIEW

After shoveling out piles of information and gaining so much knowledge, you probably feel like you are swimming in terminology and can't remember where to start. The best way to retain knowledge is through repetition, and having a quick reference guide is never a bad idea. The following pages are a brief overview of the in-depth discussions in this book, allowing you to quickly refer to a topic in a pinch.

Basic trade

A stock is a shareholding in a corporation that varies in value according to the desire or need for goods or services of that particular corporation. As a shareholder, your net worth rises and falls based on taking a short position (selling) when values are high and a long position (buying) when prices are low. As long as the stock or security is in your possession, the change in value is considered unrealized gain or loss because you cannot measure it in liquid assets (cash).

When most commodities traded in the market are on a strong upward trend for a period of time, it is called a bull market. If the value takes a sharp downward swing and continues on this path, it is called a bear market. If no such trend is recognized and the value of stocks and shares is fairly uniform, it is called a flat market.

The foreign exchange market

The Foreign Exchange Market is the exchange on which different countries in different time zones trade their domestic and international commodities in various currencies. Currency is the denomination or currency division used in a particular country (such as the U.S. dollar or the euro). When multiple currencies are in use, they are typically expressed as a ratio called a cross rate that shows the amount of a second currency that is equivalent to the first listed. Determining what the equivalent is is called currency conversion.

Several European countries, which have now consolidated their currencies to agree on the Euro (since 1999) trade on Forex, as it is called for short. Britain, which has so far chosen to continue using the pound, also participates in international trade, as do the United States, Japan and Australia. Each of these countries uses its own currency for standard business purposes, with options to invest in foreign currencies. Determining whether or not this is worthwhile depends on the currency conversion rate.

The value of a nation's currency is determined by its government and its federal bank (the Federal Reserve, better known as the FED, is the federal bank of the United States). The intentional change in the conversion rate by a government is called valuation-- devaluation is taking value and strength away from the currency, while revaluation adds strength and purchasing power to the currency. If the same change in conversion rate occurs naturally through events and market volatility, it is referred to as appreciation and devaluation.

Careers in the market

Without the assistance of professionals, it is almost impossible to trade in the open market. Market analysts follow stock market trends that influence the value of stocks. They use such information and basic history to help predict the outcome of different aspects of the market in the future.

Other individuals, called chartists, create charts that interpret all the data-various numbers, statistics, percentages, etc.-into an easy-to-read candlestick chart that plots the trends of specific commodities in the market.

A stockbroker is an individual or company that assists you in making your investments. A broker can help you make smart financial decisions by helping you track your orders and follow market trends.

A market-maker does the same job as a stockbroker, except that this individual or company maintains an investment in a particular variety of stocks and bonds that can be sold in a short time to a client at a lower price so that the client can make money by immediately selling the same stocks at the higher market price.

Other individuals can assist with loans, allowing you to buy on the margin. This involves the opposite approach-borrowing money to buy a stock or security that is at a low market value so that the customer can then resell the commodity at a higher price.

Protect your investments

There are several ways to protect your investments. By placing limit orders, you guarantee to the best of your ability that you will not lose money in the market and virtually guarantee at least a minimum profit. However, if you change your mind about these limits, you can always place a stop order. If you leave standing instructions with your stockbroker, these are called open orders that remain so until the transaction is executed and the order filled.

Try to set your limit orders just above the support levels (the lowest levels of value to which a stock can fall) and just below the resistance level (the upper level above which the value of a stock is unlikely to rise).

Also, set a value date-a date when you can take an average of the value of a particular commodity and review your options. This should be reviewed at least every six months if you plan to maintain holdings of a particular stock.

CHAPTER 13: ONE LAST OPTION

While "Chapter 13" is not an appropriate way to end a financial venture, it is, in this case, one of the most important conclusions of an incredibly useful tool full of investment advice, especially when it is placed at the end of a book to offer assistance to those threatened with bankruptcy due to bad investment decisions. There are always ways to turn back when you have started walking down the wrong path. Just like upgrading to a new car after buying a crappy car that has been nothing but a nightmare, it is possible to reverse direction.

Some people can spend days, months and even years trying to conquer the stock market and still fail. In some cases, it is virtually impossible for an individual to understand the functionality of the market. If you are unable to follow market trends, then it is better that you do not make any investment decisions.

It is okay not to adapt to the market. At the same time, you can still make money from investments. A final option you have is to create a discretionary account. This means that you sign a contract with your stockbroker and hand the agent a sum of money to invest, leaving the determination of the placement of that investment in the hands of your agent. You will never have to worry again that you have made a bad investment. In fact, in this scenario, you will not even have to follow market trends or other information having to do with financial investment. Your broker will simply let you know when you have increased your net worth or if your assets have taken a plunge.

Whatever choices you make regarding entry into the stock market, you need not worry about not having the essential information to help you through your first trading experiences. Now, you have the basic knowledge and essential reference guide to begin the path to success and wealth that you can access at any time.

Resources

1) Million Dollar Pips - The first true million dollar forex robot. Use a unique scalping strategy to bring in fast pips with literally less than 5 pip stop loss!

2) Forex MegaDroid Robot - Automatic, 100% hands free Forex Robot uses Rcpta technology and breaks all records!!!

3) Forex Growth Bot - Forex Growth Bot is a low-risk reward robot with nearly a year of trading trials, plus detailed backtests. Watch how we grow our account exponentially!

FOREX TRADING

INTRODUCTION

Forex (FX) is an acronym for Foreign Exchange, and thus Forex trading refers to the trading of currencies of different countries against each other.

With over $2 trillion of trade per day, Forex is the largest market in the world, surpassing the stock market, and the best part is that it is open 24 hours a day!

How to make money in Forex? The Forex trader generates profits by speculating whether one currency will rise or fall relative to the other.

Start by choosing a currency pair that you expect to change in value and place your order. For example, you spent $1,600 to buy 1,000 pounds today.

A few months later, if the value of pounds against the dollar increases, say 1,000 pounds against $2,000, you would earn $400 when you choose to end the trade. Alternatively, you can also hold the currency pair for minutes or days, depending on your strategy.

It is commonly thought that the best opportunities to make money are with the most commonly traded currencies, namely the U.S. dollar, Euro, British pound, Swiss franc, Japanese yen, Canadian dollar, and

Australian dollars, known collectively as the "Majors."

Although historically available only to large financial institutions and corporations, Forex is now accessible to members of the public due to the prevalence of the Internet and thus, is a good opportunity for investors to grow their money.

Contrary to common notion, you do not need a lot of money to start trading Forex. Some people even start with as little as $200.

While there are people who make a living relying solely on Forex trading, it is important to be realistic with your expectations, especially if you are a beginner. As easy as it sounds, learning the correct strategies and practicing paper trading before using real money can save you from losing your hard earned money.

After all, no investment is risk-free, and it is how you manage risk that makes the difference.

Learn the basics of Forex trading

Are you looking for the place to invest your capital? Don't worry now. There is the financial market where you can invest profitably. There are many large companies that trade in this more liquid and volatile market and earn profits with both hands.

If you like to adopt a trading career, thanks to forex trading. It is the best place to invest. Unlike many other stock markets, forex trading is the most appropriate place to invest because it operates 24 hours a day. It has a global presence, and you can also trade through electronic means such as the Internet or even with your cell phone.

For those who are new to forex trading it is simply the buying and selling of currency. It is not as simple as it seems. It involves a lot of technicalities. It is necessary to learn a lot about forex trading before entering. In this article we emphasize learning forex trading.

Today, entering the forex trading market is no longer a challenge. No need to go to the real foreign exchange market, you can access forex trading on the Internet.

There are many software programs available online that will provide you with timely market updates, currency quotes, rise and fall in currency value, and so on. The software will analyze and tell you when to buy or sell a currency.

It is recommended to gather as much information as possible before starting trading in the foreign exchange market. You should know the tricks of the trade to earn more profit. You can learn forex trading through experience and practice. Investing in forex trading and mastering it is no child's play. The more you enter the forex market, the more you will be an experienced player in this market.

Although forex trading is a great place to make money but on the contrary it becomes very expensive with a wrong move.

The last thing is when you have to trade in the Forex market. Because the Forex market is open 24/7, you can trade at any time that is convenient for you and you can get out of it whenever you want. You just have to anticipate the market trend.

Compared with bonds and stocks, forex trading is riskier. But it is more volatile and you can make billions of dollars in seconds.

Forex trading is not only for large companies and organizations. This market is open to everyone. The only conditions are that you should have sufficient capital and an account to deal in forex trading. You can opt for forex trading as a part-time task. You can trade anytime you want.

You should have the right system for trading. Get the free version of the system before you get it. Analyze the system through customer blogs and testimonials on how the system works.

Last but not least is the selection of an experienced and well-respected forex broker. He can provide you with many tips for dealing in the forex market and how to maximize your profit with increasing risk.

CHAPTER 1: FOREX TRADING KNOWLEDGE AND EDUCATION

The Foreign Exchange, also known as Forex, has become the largest liquid financial market in the world.

It has no particular location, as exchanges take place by means of an electronic network, thus involving the whole world.

Forex is not a sophisticated market, but you need to consider certain aspects if you want your trades to be successful. You can really earn large amounts of money, as many people have done and become rich overnight.

At the same time, one should always keep in mind that risks are also involved. You need to be properly educated and have adequate knowledge of Forex trading before you start actual trading.

Many of the business schools in the United States have courses on trading and financial markets. Taking such courses will only benefit you, as they provide you with the knowledge and skills you need to enter the Forex market and trade successfully.

A good business school will teach you how to read charts correctly and spot trends correctly. Reading a chart gives you insight into the direction in which a certain currency is heading.

Thus, you will be able to decide which currency to trade with. Reading a chart correctly is the skill you need most in the Forex market. It helps you reduce the risk of losing your money and increase your chances of making money.

When deciding on a particular school, you should consider those that provide real-time trading on model and even real accounts. It is a fact that the best learning comes out of experience. Therefore, you should be required to create both accounts.

You need a dummy account to practice and a real account to trade. Your real account should not be large, so you will not lose much money if you make mistakes. By practicing you gain experience. You will learn more about the way Forex works, which will help you when you decide to become a real trader in the market.

Various trading systems should be available at these schools so that you can try them out and decide which one is easier for you to use. More importantly, know how these systems work and are used, for the same purpose of avoiding mistakes in the real market.

Due to the fact that it is largely based on speculation, Forex is indeed a risky market. You must have a knowledge of the market and the skills to trade on it. You can earn money very easily, but at the same time you can lose it instantly. You need to be properly educated before you start trading in this market.

Nowadays anyone who owns a computer and has an Internet connection can trade Forex. You should keep in mind the fact that Forex cannot guarantee winning for everyone.

The more knowledge you have, the greater your chances of making a profit in Forex trading. It is better not to intervene if you only think you can. Inform yourself first.

How to get ahead in the game of Forex trading

Nowadays every company is facing fierce competition. Companies pay millions of dollars to enter their exact target market.

While there is a market that pays you to know.

It is forex trading. Forex trading is the recent name for the foreign exchange market, where the buying and selling of currencies takes place.

Before indulging in forex trading, you should have a complete understanding of the FX market. You should be aware of trading strategies and tactics, market trends, and factors affecting currency value.

Research is the most important element of forex trading. To get comprehensive information about forex trading you should attend trading courses and training programs or act as a broker's assistant.

Forex training courses allow you to familiarize yourself with the language of trading. It also makes you understand the trends in the foreign exchange market. It also tells you what is the perfect time to buy and sell currency.

These training courses help you cope with immense challenges, high currency demand and market stress. They also equip you to handle unwanted circumstances with patience.

In forex training classes you will learn to analyze the market that when buying and selling currency is advantageous and profitable. You will also learn how to deal with software and other tools.

Trading courses help you do financial and fundamental market analysis. In addition to theory, forex trading courses make you understand the psychology of trading and money management. Everything you need Forex trading courses allow you to enter the foreign exchange market practically through an internship.

These courses offer avenues such as conferences with traders that will make you learn through real-time examples. With the help of these practical experiences, discussions and information you will be able to fully understand foreign exchange.

The Internet is a more efficient source of learning today. There are many websites that offer online forex trading courses at an optimal price. You can learn risk and money management, financial and technical market analysis, trading strategies and tactics.

You can also participate in online classes on modern software and tools used in foreign markets. They also facilitate lifetime subscription programs to learn more about the latest market trends and strategies to cope with these changing market conditions.

Every day there is a new innovation; online services allow you to learn new ways to manage changing market trends. As the number of online trading institutions is increasing rapidly, this makes it easier for you to learn about more ways to earn profits. It is possible to have a complete track of the value of currencies and business directories on the Internet.

Moreover, it is said that the literate and the illiterate can never be the same. Similarly, one cannot succeed in forex trading without learning the language of the market, its trends, currency analysis, and financial and technical analysis of the FX market.

Learning will make you perfect speculators who can approach any situation wisely and can minimize losses while earning maximum profit with proper implementation of strategies and tactics.

CHAPTER 2: EVALUATE THE RIGHT TIME TO INVEST

To trade successfully in Forex, you must be able to understand the trading signals that can contribute greatly to your profits.
Select a chart that describes these trading indicators and rationally opt for a trading system that can maximize the benefit of these trading indicators.

These signals can help make important decisions regarding market entry and exit or to make any adjustments in currency exchange.

Technical indicators describe the facts and figures of trading by making certain mathematical calculations and indicate the time period that was selected for the calculation of these indicators. Charts in Forex show continuously updated exchange rates of various currencies, upward or downward trends, and technical indicators.

Each graph is updated after a specified period of time. It is necessary to know these charts and technical indicators before making an investment.

It is a sensible rule to consult charts before entering the foreign exchange market. One can also consult multiple charts to understand the best time to enter. After mastering the evaluation of entry signals, it is necessary to pay attention to exit signals.

Consider many trailing stop options, fixed stops, and limited exits that you can use for your exit. If you plan to trade short, try to focus on "turning points" by understanding any short-term patterns that may repeat in the long run.

Monitor currency pairs to understand any such fluctuations. Traders usually prefer to set a higher percentage for a short period, opting for the limit exit.

You can also consult exit signals that are based on real-time transactions to make a decision about your exit.

In addition to carefully consulting technical indicators, you must use a signal that best suits your conditions. Instead of making a random decision you have to stick to a logical mechanism. Try using multiple signals in accordance with many parameters that will lead you to risk aversion.

Evaluating various Forex signals along with technical indicators allows you to control your investment and anticipate possible market fluctuations.

Forex trading requires strict attention and observation, and any negligence can result in great losses. Technological advances have made it possible to analyze the foreign exchange market 24 hours a day through the Internet.

You can also buy and sell currency over the phone, because the need for physical presence has been eliminated in modern Forex trading.

Nowadays, if Forex trading indicators meet the defined parameters, you will receive an alert to invest or sell your shares. To ensure the highest possible return on your investment, decide to follow trading signals from an experienced service provider.

You need to find the best trading system for you. Logical evaluation of figures and signals allows you to grasp the right opportunity. It is necessary to conduct thorough research before making a transaction and not rely only on one source.

Read reviews, online trading forums, newspapers and business magazines on foreign exchange to deeply understand the underlying system of foreign exchange trading.

Use software to evaluate signals or a method developed by any foreign exchange expert. Take notes and discover the right trading system that works for you.

Forex Trading: Finding the right moment
The Forex or Foreign exchange market is currently the largest financial market in the world where any vigilant person can earn huge profits.

Although forex is so vulnerable that it can turn profits into losses in no time, currency trading continues 24 hours (excluding weekends).

It allows international traders to conduct their business smoothly, regardless of the disparity of currencies among different regions of the world. Because of the volume of currency exchange, which amounts to trillions of dollars a day, forex can bring good fortune to money traders around the world.

Fluctuation in currency exchange rates can easily undermine a trader's opportunity for profit. One must realize that forex trading is more of an art than mere luck.

Familiarize yourself with the tactics of this risky game and understand the basic rules that can lead to huge gains. One important factor that can contribute heavily to your profits is the right time to sell or buy currency in forex.

Due to the time difference between different regions of the world, trading activity does not remain at its peak 24 hours. There is an optimal time when the maximum number of buyers and sellers gather for currency exchange.

You must be aware of the importance of these "rush hours" during which trading volume explodes, making forex the most liquid market in the world.

The exchange rate of currencies is not fixed, as in banks and other financial institutions. Currencies are traded at a floating exchange rate and trade in pairs such as dollar/euro, euro/pound.

One must be very cautious because of the uncertainty about the rates of various currencies, as current business and rumors can greatly affect the value of a currency.

According to Eastern Standard Time, Forex starts working at 5:00 p.m. on Sunday until 4:00 p.m. Nearly 85 percent of traders deal in major currencies. The trading cycle starts in New Zealand and expands to Australia and Asia.

The Middle East then joins the foreign exchange market followed by Europe. Eventually America participates in trading. Developed countries that have strong economies play a vital role in international forex with major currency trading centers in New York, Tokyo and London.

All experienced currency traders know that there is a specific time in forex when all the markets in the world take part in the activity.

When Europe and America are stimulated during Asia's functional hours, trading volume reaches billions of dollars.

Due to a large number of currency buyers and sellers are available during these hours, capital becomes highly liquid and exchange rates are determined.

You must have a table describing forex working hours in different countries. In Australia, currency exchange starts at 7 p.m., according to

Eastern Standard Time and continues until 3 a.m. At 3 am, Forex in Britain opens for business and closes at 11 am. London forex operating hours are from 2 a.m. until 12 noon. New York City hours are from 8 a.m. to 4 p.m. EST.

As for Tokyo, currency is bought and sold from 8 p.m. to 4 a.m. All these times are listed according to Eastern Standard Time. If you draw a diagram, you will realize that during 2 a.m. and 4 a.m. the open markets of Asia and Europe work simultaneously.

Similarly, during 8 a.m.-12 p.m. EST, American and European currency exchange activities coincide. By taking these peak business hours into consideration, one can be sure to reach the maximum number of traders worldwide and thus the chances of earning high profits increase manifold.

CHAPTER 3: FOREIGN EXCHANGE MARKET

We all earn professional degrees and pursue careers to make our futures secure.

To realize all wishes and dreams, we need sufficient resources that can help us access life's luxuries. Well, this power is called money, which can make your life easier by providing comfort and facilities.

Professionals and employers earn enough money on average to cover all expenses, but they cannot even expect to take a dream vacation or buy luxury cars or ostentatious jewelry.

Because you will not be able to escape heavy debt later. So consider earning money in addition to your regular job or a small business and invest your savings to earn profits without spending your time and energy.

Instead of dumping your money into bank savings accounts that always offer a fixed rate of return over a given period, try something that is undoubtedly risky but can bring you luck. This opportunity is

called Forex, where foreign currencies are bought and sold 24 hours a day. Now, if you are thinking that international traders usually trade currency in Forex, then what do you have to do with that? The technique is simple. You just need to understand the rules of trading and exchange, the timing and rate of exchange.

If you are able enough to judge the right time to buy a currency whose value is down at the moment but is expected to rise in the near future, you can earn huge gains at Forex.

One foreign currency is bought by giving another in exchange, so trade takes place in foreign currency pairs. Currencies of developed countries are traded more frequently than others. The favorites are the U.S., Japan, and England, which ultimately regard the currency pairs of these countries as important.

The U.S. dollar with the pound sterling, the U.S. dollar with the Japanese yen, the U.S. dollar with the Swiss franc, and the pound sterling with the U.S. dollar are the most traded currency pairs in Forex.

The downside of investing in Forex is the risk involved that can drain your investment due to fluctuations in currency prices. When conditions are right, it is possible to achieve a 100 percent rate of return on investment.

But if the asset is low or the value of the currency falls, you will have to bear a huge loss because the margin of loss is equal to the margin of gain. Thus, Forex can be a financial disaster for you if you are not in control of the trading mechanism and tactics.

You must invest your surplus money in the foreign exchange market and be fully aware of possible market fluctuations. As they say 'no gain without pain' Forex is a dynamic trading opportunity.

If you do not want to save time or energy to examine Forex continuously, you can hire a stockbroker or financial analyst who is experienced in these transactions.

Even then you must be able to read and understand forex rates, market trends, options to call, and all the other terminology and structure of international foreign exchange markets. Read articles and online tutorials that will improve your forex knowledge and point out various rules of the largest liquid financial market. Keep one thing in mind, investing in forex is not a game of chance, rather it is a technical, difficult but profitable game.

Trading sul forex: Huge opportunities

The largest financial market where foreign currency is bought and sold is called Forex, denoted Fx. International traders and financial institutions such as banks and brokerage firms and large corporations usually trade currencies and invest huge funds in Forex.

Because of a large number of buyers and sellers around the world, Forex is considered the largest liquid capital market. Fx trading amounts to trillions of dollars a day and is constantly monitored by financial analysts and brokers around the world.

Exchange rate fluctuation is mainly enjoyed by large investment banks and government financial institutions that buy huge amounts of a specific currency in order to sell it at higher prices in the future.

Technological advances have enabled the world to stay connected around the clock and exchange currency whenever conditions are suitable for trade. Anyone can now find comprehensive information about Forex and financial market trends to discover the right strategies before making an investment.

Countries with strong economies and infrastructure play an important role in Forex with the currencies of the United States, Great Britain, Canada, Japan and Australia traded most frequently. Currency trading in Forex stops only on weekends and continues 24 hours every working day.

The greatest advantage of FX is the immense geographic dispersion that allows the sale and purchase of currency across borders, via the Internet and telephone.

To date, Forex has gained international acceptance and importance for foreign exchange and does not fix the rate of any currency. Rather, a currency is purchased at a fluctuating exchange rate that is determined by

The perceived value of any currency and the willingness of the parties to hold it. Earning profits at Forex is easier than the conventional way, where you do not have to produce or trade any goods. You just need to have knowledge, experience and investment funds.

Among the many advantages of investing in Forex, the main one is easily liquidated capital due to a large number of brokers and investors available all day long. You will always find a buyer or seller for any type of currency anywhere in the world. This is the reason for a huge trading volume in Forex, which is $1.5 million per day.

In addition, Forex investing is a technical and practical game, and there are no hidden rules or intricate trading procedures. Past and current data are available to study trends and patterns in exchange rates, and future forecasting and analysis can be done through various software or by observing the current affairs of a specific country.

You can sell or buy currency literally throughout the day. Just view the operating hours if you want to trade with a specific forex country. Many brokers have made it possible for small investors to invest money.

You can control your money invested with high leverage in Forex, and you can have a leverage rate as high as 1:400, which means you will earn

$400 for every dollar invested in your account. You can sell your currency directly to the buyer without paying any middleman.

Only if you incorporate some brokers for financial assistance will you then have to pay a certain percentage. With sound knowledge and keen observation and effective research, one can earn a fortune by investing in the foreign exchange market. Find the right trading system for you and take advantage of specialized software designed to unravel exchange rate trends.

CHAPTER 4: AUTOMATE FOREX TRADING

The current era is witnessing a technological boom that brings about many changes at all levels of knowledge and human beings.

Trade has not been left untouched. Everyone trades in one way or another. It has become a must for survival. You can cope with the modern world only if you are open-minded, efficient and hardworking.

People trade all sorts of things, sometimes not even realizing that they are actually involved in such an activity. The best example is Forex trading.

Individuals often trade currencies, even if they do not think of it as such. If they were aware of this, they would know that they can earn seriously. And it became so accessible.

What was once the exclusive area of corporations is now within reach of almost everyone, especially with the increasing use of the Internet. All over the world people are trading online. They can also trade Forex

online, no matter whether rich or not, as long as they are connected to the Internet. This kind of business requires fairly simple things, such as a secure system that is used to produce signals.

These automatically generated signals can provide you with the much-desired opportunity to hit the currency market. You can get them from any kind of media, be it television, newspapers, internet forums.

However, there is a risk that the signals you get are sometimes distorted. To avoid this, you must be able to choose balanced automatic signals without bias.

To get these signals, it is vital for you to have the right system, that particular software that is designed for the purpose of Forex trading. You can find many systems on the Internet. As you might expect, they are not free, but you can try the trial version.

Here you have reached the most important step. You must be absolutely sure that you have selected the best system before you buy it. You must be aware that there are people who will try to convince you to buy their software, a system that will not work for a single second.

It is advisable that you make your selection from that list of systems that have been on the market for some years, which have established a reputation in this area. You can get an idea of these systems simply by doing some research on the Internet or participating in online discussions.

Now that you have the system, you can proceed to the next step, that of subscribing to automatic alerts regarding Forex trading. Now you are ready to receive alerts and go into business.

These automatic signals alert you to the entry and exit value of major currencies. You know in real time where the euro is against the U.S. dollar, so you can trade accordingly all day, all week.

Whenever there is a change for trading, you receive an alert. It can be sent to your e-mail or cell phone. These alerts really help you make the wisest decision regarding your Forex trading.

Automated Forex trading strategy

Having an automated Forex trading system can give you an advantage in Forex trading, but having a Forex strategy can give you an edge. If you want to reap long-term profits, then don't trade using your instincts or just because a particular trade excites you.

You need a trading system or strategy to make sure you get solid transactions and trades.

A Forex strategy or system consists of rules that guide you on how to trade in the Forex market. A Forex strategy or system provides information on when to enter a trade and how to exit it. It would also enable you to apply and use risk management rules.

There are ways to know if your Forex trading strategy is really successful or good:

- Begin to know how successful it has been in the past. It pays to know how much previous or existing users of the system have earned so far using the strategy.

In addition to this, you also get some information about how much is the maximum drawdown of the system in its previous trading.

- There is a win/loss ratio that you can also control. It is about how much you have won compared to how much you have lost. In addition to this, there is also a profit/loss ratio. This relates to the average of winning versus losing exchanges.
- You should also know how consistent the system is in providing profits.

When choosing a Forex strategy, one should not only consider the success rate and profit percentage. You should also consider your lifestyle and what system can be used to suit or satisfy it. You should know which Forex trading system can be used appropriately in your time zone.

A useful strategy used in Forex trading is what is called leverage. With the leverage strategy, you would earn about one hundred times the amount of money you are trading in your account.

Many traders have testified that they have been able to win many profits using this type of strategy. So if you have a funded Forex account, you can use this strategy to make more profit.

Another strategy is the stop-loss order. This strategy works by identifying a point at which you will not trade. This trading point is identified and determined before trading begins.

When using this type of strategy, you should be able to analyze the trading signals so that you do not miss your prediction. If your planned trade has not progressed as you expected, the stop loss system could be very disadvantageous.

Automated Forex trading is another type of system or strategy. The entry and exit of an order will be determined by the automated system. Again, the price and point at which the program will enter or exit a trade is predetermined.

These Forex trading strategies would help you have better trading opportunities in the Forex market. Whether you are using leverage, stop loss or automated Forex trading system and strategies, 100% success is not guaranteed.

These strategies are not intended to give you perfect trades, because that is impossible. These trading strategies are here to help us minimize the risk of losing in trading.

Advantages of automated Forex trading system

Forex trading has one of the largest market shares in the world. It earns about $3 trillion each year worldwide. But Forex trading is primarily speculative; profits and losses are based on the movement of the currency.

The large round of profits attracts many investors. Even those who are still starting out in this field are interested in joining, to make it easier, there is an automated Forex trading system that could help them make the transition easier.

With an automated Forex trading system, you would have a programmed system that could monitor the progress of Forex trading in real time. It uses an expert advisor and a set of indicators that interprets Forex trade and can also show a trade opportunity.

What is good about using an automated Forex trading system is the quick way to catch things. If you are a newcomer to trading, this would minimize the long process of learning the market and its rules.

It is not necessary to stay glued to the Forex market 24 hours to understand the Forex trading market. The software would keep track of trade 24 hours a day.

This would keep you abreast of what is happening in real time. This would allow you to make changes to your account in real time based on changes occurring in the market. Major changes in trading could happen in a matter of seconds.

Apart from that, the automatic Forex trading system gets rid of the emotional and psychological aspect of trading. There would be times when a series of losses can affect the way you think about and analyze the market.

This could lead to wrong and rash decisions in the market. But the automated Forex trading system and software would help you deal with it.

The software is also easy to use and simple to install. You can let it go on autopilot. Setting up the software takes only a few minutes, and then you can let it do its work and magic.

You can be successful in automatic Forex trading especially if you use a system that is suitable for you and at the same time, you are familiar with.

This would also allow you to be flexible and have a diversified Forex trade. The automatic Forex trading system can work with different types of brokers and different types of currencies. You will be able to trade with different markets and currencies. You can trade while on the road.

But the automatic Forex trading system is not perfect. If it were, then many people would be winning the trade. Money management is still important. You have to know how much you are willing to risk.

To be successful, most traders would always have a fixed percentage of their capital at risk. They could increase the size of their trade if they win or decrease if they lose.

If you already have an automated Forex trading system, then it would be best not to make any changes to the settings or configurations. Having an automated Forex trading system does not guarantee success. Nor is it the only thing you should rely on to be successful in trading.

There are some factors that can affect trade. The Forex market changes very quickly depending on various factors and situations. In addition to having an automated Forex trading system, the investor or trader must also have knowledge of the trading system.

Risks of automated Forex trading system

We have heard how great the automated Forex trading system is. There are numerous advantages to using it. But is it only about positive things? There are two sides to a coin, so what is the other side of an automated Forex trading system?

Some traders and investors would say that intuition means a lot in trading. Some would say it played an important role when they closed a deal or when they won in an exchange. But some traders would say that intuition does not play a role.

Some would say it works for them, while others would dispute it. But since some people rely on intuition to get good trades, an automated system would not be able to help them. Because programs and computers are not based on intuition at all.

Another common thing that traders using an automated Forex trading system do is to have their computers and programs take their place in trading. Actually, this is a great idea.

Having a machine that does your job for you by making you take care of other matters. But this turns into a disadvantage especially when you let the program and the computer do ALL the work.

It is very easy to be comfortable with this configuration, relying too much on your own software. In fact, even systems can make mistakes. You would also need to recognize opportunities and at the same time trade on-hand.

Another downside of an automated Forex trading system is making sure that your computer is always running and that you have a dedicated server to run your automated trading. This is to make sure that your expert advisors or EAs work with your home and work computers.

There would be times when you would encounter a graphical pattern or wave analysis that is very difficult to do. So, you will have to find professionals to interpret your charts for you and decode some extremely difficult patterns.

Another truth you should face is that not all experienced consultants easily handle errors and other contingencies. Therefore, you should prepare for anything that might disappoint you.

Not everything is perfect. So, you should be prepared to face disappointments and handle them. This is why you would still need knowledge in manual Forex trading.

Nothing is perfect; even computers and programs still make mistakes and can have difficulty dealing with unexpected and crucial points in trading. Traders and investors prefer to use both automated systems and manual trading. They would use an automated trading system if they find manual trading difficult. Whereas, systems as simple as simple graphic patterns are left to be done manually.

Besides all this, another downside is that automatic Forex trading is too popular on the Internet. This can be good or bad. The good thing is that getting an automated system is easy and within reach.

While the bad thing is that too much popularity can cause numerous websites to come up with scams and cheats on the Internet.

There are many automatic Forex trading systems for sale on the Internet. They claim that their products are the best among systems, but they fail to meet standards. That is why it is recommended to check customer reviews and have a money-back guarantee for your purchase.

Using Forex trading software

Money is always needed. Almost all the things we must have or use to live must be paid for. In fact, "many makes the world go around," as the song says. It is no wonder, then, that there are systems in place to enable global currency trade.

The world's largest financial market, Forex works with thousands of millions of dollars worldwide, 24 hours a day, seven days a week. A real trader would know that this market can seriously increase his income and would consider getting involved in the business.

There is already software at your fingertips to help you develop your Forex trading through automatic selling and buying of currency by you. Fortunately, the range of choices is quite wide, so you can select any software you want.

There are also websites that upon signing up provide you with free trading software, a bonus to set up a Forex account on them.

Sometimes it is just the demo version, and most likely you have to pay for the real thing.

Different types of currency trading software can be accessed on the Internet. It is recommended to try the demos first and see which is easier to use, and then purchase the full version. As a currency trader, it is vital to have an automatic for your Forex transactions.

There are basically two types of software: web-based and desktop-based. It is your choice which program you need, and it is always you who knows how comfortable you feel when you use a certain software for your exchanges.

Regardless of what kind of software you have decided to rely on, you should know that Internet speed is essential. It is extremely important that your Internet connection be high-speed, so as to keep you away from any information lag, which could otherwise result in a financial catastrophe.

Software that is desktop-based operates with data stored on the computer's hard drive. Even if the information is on the disk, it is necessary to protect that disk from any possible accidents, viruses, or hacks.

It is strongly recommended that only one computer be used for currency trading. There are also computers designed specifically for this purpose, but they are quite expensive.

Web-based software differs in that security should be the responsibility of the vendor. It is more convenient to use, since there is no need to download any software. In addition, you can manage your Forex transactions from anywhere in the world. You just need an Internet connection to access your account.

In addition to these differences, there is also a price. While the desktop type pays only once when you purchase the software, the web-based type requires a monthly fee for system maintenance.

There are advantages and disadvantages to each type of software. Neither is good or bad. The one that fits your needs is the best for you. It is important, however, to have automated Forex trading software that provide real-time access to data and changes in the market.

CHAPTER 5: FOREX BEGINNER - HOW TO OPEN A FOREX ACCOUNT

Unlike the stock market, Forex trading does not take place in a physical location nor does it have a central exchange. Thus, a Forex trader can trade wherever he or she is, 24 hours a day for

5.5 days a week! It is no wonder that Forex trading is so attractive to many new investors. To begin Forex trading, you must first open an online trading account where all currency transactions will take place.

Opening a Forex account involves three simple steps:

- Choosing an appropriate Forex trading site.
There are two things to consider when choosing the right Forex trading site for you. The first is the leverage the site offers. Each site offers different leverage, which can range from 50:1 up to 250:1.

A leverage factor of 50:1, for example, would allow a person with $1,000 in his account to trade $50,000 in the Forex market. While this could allow you to make large gains with small investments, it can also amplify your losses if a trade moves against you.

It is important to understand the risks involved in determining the leverage you intend to use. In addition, the trading site should be commission-free, as there is no need to go through a third party, such as brokers for stocks.

Examine the site well before deciding to make sure it offers the features you need.

- Choose a suitable type of account

Forex trading accounts are available in different sizes, ranging from US$25 (micro/mini accounts) to US$10,000 (standard accounts). Choose the size of the account according to the amount you want to invest.

Choose the spot Forex trading account, which allows instant trades and is more popular, instead of a futures account.

- Register for a Forex trading account

Most registration is done online and requires your personal and credit card information for real money exchanges. Be sure to enter your email address correctly.

- Activate your Forex trading account

You will be asked to verify your data through several steps. Be sure to read and understand the terms and conditions before signing them online. Pay particular attention to site operating hours, availability of live technical support, and any hidden fees/charges.

Some sites also offer a limited-time demo account without real money. You can use it to familiarize yourself with Forex trading before trading with real money. Congratulations! Now you are ready to hit the Forex market!

Understanding Forex jargon

One of the biggest frustrations of Forex traders is the huge amount of jargon. Googling these terms also does not seem to help, because the explanations are more often than not, they contain other jargon.

This section will explain five common technical terms used in Forex trading in layman's language.

- **Quotation:** Forex trading is always done in pairs, so one currency is always quoted against another currency, for example, USD/JPY, EUR/USD, AUD/GBP. A quotation would be like this: USD/JPY = 100.00.

The currency on the left (in this case, the U.S. dollar) is known as the "base currency" and is always equal to 1 unit, while the currency on the right (in this case, the Japanese yen) is called the quote or counter currency.

A quote is how much a unit of the base currency is worth, so this particular quote means that 1 USD can buy 100.00 Japanese yen.

- **Pip:** stands for "percentage in point" which is the smallest trade increment in Forex. Prices in the Forex market are always quoted to the fourth decimal place, except for the Japanese Yen; for example, when EUR/USD rises from 1.5200 to 1.5201, it goes up 1 pip.

For the Japanese Yen, 1 pip is equivalent to 0.01 (two decimal places). Most currency pairs trade between 100 and 150 pips per day.

- **Bid / Ask:** In Forex, making a bid means "buying" while "asking" means "selling." The quote on the left is the bid (buy) price while the quote on the right is the ask (sell) price, and the bid price is always lower than the ask price. The base currency would be the currency in which the transaction would be conducted.

Let's look at the example, EUR/USD 1.2600/02. Selling this currency pair means selling the base currency, which is the EURO. The market would buy your 1 EURO of base currency with 1.2600 USD. In contrast, to buy 1 EURO, you need 1.2602 Japanese yen.

- **Spread:** is the difference between the bid price and the ask price. Using the same example as above, the spread was 2 pips, which you automatically pay to your broker on each trade.

- **Margin:** The minimum amount of money required to make a trade with a broker. You can trade as long as your account has this minimum amount, otherwise your accounts would be closed.

Understanding the terminologies would definitely boost your trading confidence and discuss your trading with other traders without sounding like a total novice!

CHAPTER 6: SUCCESSFUL STRATEGIES FOR FULL-TIME FOREX TRADERS

If you have just started your home Internet business as a full-time forex trader and are a little confused about how to earn good profits from the forex market, then this chapter is for you.

Starting a home-based business on the Internet as a forex trader is very easy. You just need a PC with an Internet connection, a forex account and forex trading software. Earning regular profits from the forex market is your main goal, and you need to plan your strategies accordingly to achieve your main goal.

The full-time forex trader must know the forex market very well. It is not possible to know and learn in a single day. It is the process and you have to enter into this process to be successful in the forex market. First try to gather as much information as possible from different sources related to the forex market.

Then search for the best forex trading course for you and learn the different critical situations in the forex market and what to do when. Once you finish the forex course, test your knowledge and trade using dummy forex accounts. Dummy forex accounts are a forex beginner's best friend.

Here you will find real forex market situations to test your skills without any risk involvement since you are not playing with real money. Once you practice with dummy forex accounts, it is time to get the right forex trading account and platform for your forex trading.

It can be done by getting the right forex brokers who will help you in all your forex trading activities.

You must take help from forex alerts, but your source of forex alerts must be reliable and trustworthy. Forex alerts help you make the right decision and sometimes help you check your forecasts with forecasts from forex market experts, which help you increase your confidence in the forex market.

You must take the help of forex technical analysis for all your complex trades in the forex market.

Successful strategies for part-time Forex traders

The Forex market is a money market. Millions and millions of people come every day to try their luck. Some of them succeed in the market, while others fail. Those who succeed love the style of business and make it their regular source of income, while those who fail leave the forex market and never return.

When I ask myself the question: what is the reason for success and failure in the forex market? I find only one answer: strategy. The right strategy makes a man successful while following the wrong strategy makes him fail in the forex market. Here we are going to discuss successful strategies for part-time forex traders.

As we all know, part time forex traders are those who can only provide a little time of their day or week to the forex market and want to earn good profits in the forex market. Therefore, they must plan their strategies accordingly and execute them correctly to succeed in the market.

They must use the automated forex platform instead of the regular forex platform for their forex trading activities. The automated forex platform saves the trader's time by automatically generating trade at the best possible trading conditions in the market and also earns steady money on a regular basis for the trader in the forex market.

Most part-time forex traders are taking the help of forex alerts for their trades in the forex market. The forex alert is the paid or free advice from forex experts to forex traders to execute trade in the forex market.

You must get forex alert and it must be from a reliable and trusted source. You can make the best use of your automated forex platform by combining it with reliable forex alerts to get better results in the forex market.

CHAPTER 7: 34 TIPS FOR TRADING FOREX SUCCESSFULLY

Undoubtedly, trading involves much more than what is contained in a few brief tips.
A solid trading system is needed, augmented by experience, a courageous spirit and, of course, capital.

But, for most people who are just starting to trade, and for others who may be losing their joy and confidence because of large, but hopefully temporary, declines in market values, a basic overview can restore clarity to your trading.

With this in mind, some suggestions are presented that we hope will help you navigate these exciting financial waters:

1. If a position shows negative activity, do not increase risk by entering deeper.

This is the same as the old saying of traders: "Never add to a losing trade."

2. Never fail to decide on a stop and profit target before entering a trade. Use your knowledge of the market to determine stop placement, not the amount of money you have available in your account. It is not possible to conduct the trade if a suitable stop is too expensive.

3. Keep in mind the privilege of a position. A market judgment should not be made when you are already in position. Once you are in a position, all your decisions to add to the position, protect the position or exit the position should already be made.

4. Sometimes circumstances change, and when you determine this, you make the choice to exit a trade. Don't assume that you can simply take your price choice with the easy plan of going out to the market.

An example of this is when a big surprise news story comes out after a big event. This can push the acceptable level of volatility beyond what works with your trading methods.

5. Don't buy a boring market in a bear market and don't sell a boring market

market in a bull market.

Simply translated, this means that if there is no momentum in one direction or the other, then there is little chance of following the trend necessary to make a profit. Enter the trades you have determined will have the greatest chance of success.

6. When the market is very volatile or is experiencing a lack of liquidity, you should not trade. Even when there is the potential for extreme volatility, caution should be used.

Although volatile market movements have the potential for huge gains, they can be too unpredictable. Always avoid unnecessary risks when trading.

7. It is important to keep in mind that the same trading systems do not always work in both upward and downward markets. If you have a trend-following Forex trading system, you must understand that there is always the possibility that it may not work admirably in sideways markets.

8. You have to adapt your trading strategy with each type of market: uptrend, range bound and down trading. Ideally, with a trend following trading system, it would be best to avoid side markets altogether.

There is nothing wrong with a trend-following system "stepping aside" during sideways markets--in fact, it is preferable for it to step aside.

9. Choose transactions that move along with the dominant market model. Although upward and downward market patterns are always distinguishable, one or the other is always the most dominant. For example, during an upward market, sell signals are repeatedly taken, only to be respectively stopped.

This all goes back to the timeless statement: "The trend is your friend." Trading in the direction with the highest probability of success is simply common sense. This is not to say that one cannot develop a countertrend trading system that can be profitable.

10. A sell signal is just a failed buy signal; a buy signal is just a failed sell signal.

11. A losing trade is always much less difficult to enter!

12. Follow your instincts; if you don't feel comfortable with something, don't trade.

13. When you hear advice about Forex trading ignore it. Go with what you know and what is the trading system in which you have had time to develop confidence.

14. Current events in the news are significant only when they do NOT push the market in the direction of the news.

15. You gain a modicum of understanding when you read yesterday's paper today, armed with knowledge of today's market activity. You realize that yesterday's market activity has no impact on today's.

16. Never make your trading decisions based on the direction of a gap. The market should not force you to make a trade.

17. Use the "get in late, get out early" rule, keeping in mind that the first and last ticks are by far the most expensive.

18. You come out when you realize everyone else is in.

19. Do not increase the risk factor by trading when you are sick. Trading can be tiring enough without the added stress of not feeling well. Avoid trading when there is something that might affect your trading discipline.

20. Your trading unit should be changed only when you have a plan of achieved goals. You should establish a reduction plan for times when the market has lower volume or your trading is a bit off.

A good money management system is part of any good trading plan. It will reduce the size of your position when your trading system is not in sync with the market and increase the size of your position when your trading system is in sync with the market.

21. Do not be conceited or boastful in any way. Enjoy your success in trading

With pride and modesty.

22. Judge your success by the growth of your capital over time, not by the success of individual trades. Even a bad trader can have a winning streak.

23. Taking a break from trading for a day often breaks a losing streak.

24. If you are on the crest of a wave, keep going! You are doing something right. Why would you want to stop? When you and your trading methods are in tune with the markets, continue your winning streak.

25. When you have an off day, turn off the computer screen and find something else to do. Don't keep working when you are losing; there is no point.

Getting away for a while is not an easy thing to do, but it is important to discipline yourself to do it.

26. Scalpers reduce the number of variables affecting market risk by being in trades or positions for only a few seconds. Day traders reduce market risk by staying in trades for minutes.

It makes perfect sense that the smaller your profit goal is, the faster it will be achieved. This is what attracted many to day trading. If this style of trading interests you, keep the following in mind:

Increased trading frequency = increased transaction costs

27. The decision to convert a scalp or day trade into a position trade means that you have not properly understood the risks of the trade.

28. Don't let an opportunity you missed bother you.

Opportunities are around every bend.

There are new opportunities every single day. So many new traders like to talk about the big money they left on the table.

Experienced traders are happy to have taken their slice of the price action. Rarely, if ever, do you get 100% of the possible profit potential of ANY trade.

29. It is better to learn how to trade Forex than to search for an elusive secret formula.

30. Do not trust the advice of others because they probably did not do as

A lot of research like you did.

This is a really striking statement. Sometimes it seems that the grass is greener on the other side of the fence. There will be days when it seems like everyone else is in the know but you. Don't let that bother you. If you have done your homework, your time will come.

31. Mentally establishing the reality of what is happening, good or bad, up or down, stating it out loud in the midst of a mind full of preconceived notions.

If you have a losing trade, don't be afraid to tell yourself: "Clearly my trading method did not work in that trade, but my research has shown me that if I continue on this path I will be successful!

32. Flexibility is absolutely necessary to be successful in day trading. You must be an informed participant, understanding the market potential for both sides of the market. An informed decision maker makes operations with an understanding of what the current market climate is.

33. Deliberate, even complain and confess your errors in discipline. It seems that you will continue to make these kinds of mistakes for many years, so reminding yourself can delay the inevitable.

34. If this list has made you uncomfortable, then you are like many other traders in two ways:

A. You have enough trading experience to understand that the mistakes are yours, not the market's, and you try to overcome these inadequacies.

B. Oddly enough, you have become one with the market. You cannot leave and you do not want to leave. Wherever you go in life, you will ALWAYS keep an eye on the market.

CONCLUSION

Forex trading can be fun and tremendously profitable, but in all honesty, it is always more fun when it is profitable.

In the examples shown you can see firsthand that Forex trading does not have to be complicated. Yes, it requires work and dedication, but all things that have enormous potential rewards require work and dedication.

The rules, tips and techniques laid out in this book are designed to lay the foundation for successful trading. Some of these are hard and fast rules that you absolutely must not ignore. Many of these rules have to do with discipline and risk control.

Without these you simply cannot succeed. Even if you are exceptionally well capitalized you can easily make your account disappear without risk control.

If you remain disciplined, properly capitalized, and risk-aware, Forex trading offers you the opportunity of a lifetime. Leverage

available in Forex combined with proper money management can grow a small trading account to capital levels you never thought possible. To your success in trading